PAINT EFFECTS
& SPECTACULAR FINISHES

PAINT EFFECTS
& SPECTACULAR FINISHES

A SIMPLE-TO-USE PRACTICAL GUIDE FOR EVERY HOME

SACHA COHEN

LORENZ BOOKS

This edition is published by Lorenz Books,
an imprint of Anness Publishing Ltd, Hermes House,
88–89 Blackfriars Road, London SE1 8HA;
tel. 020 7401 2077; fax 020 7633 9499

www.lorenzbooks.com; www.annesspublishing.com

If you like the images in this book and would like to investigate using them for publishing, promotions
or advertising, please visit our website www.practicalpictures.com for more information.

UK agent: The Manning Partnership Ltd;
tel. 01225 478444; fax 01225 478440; sales@manning-partnership.co.uk
UK distributor: Grantham Book Services Ltd;
tel. 01476 541080; fax 01476 541061; orders@gbs.tbs-ltd.co.uk
North American agent/distributor: National Book Network;
tel. 301 459 3366; fax 301 429 5746; www.nbnbooks.com
Australian agent/distributor: Pan Macmillan Australia;
tel. 1300 135 113; fax 1300 135 103; customer.service@macmillan.com.au
New Zealand agent/distributor: David Bateman Ltd;
tel. (09) 415 7664; fax (09) 415 8892

Publisher: Joanna Lorenz
Senior Editor: Toria Leitch
Project Editor: Martin Goldring
Contributing Editor: Geraldine Christy
Designer: Isobel Gillan
Photography: Lucinda Symons (projects), Rodney Forte (techniques) and John Freeman (equipment and techniques)
Stylist: Diana Civil
Production Controller: Yolande Denny

ETHICAL TRADING POLICY

At Anness Publishing we believe that business should be conducted in an ethical and ecologically sustainable
way, with respect for the environment and a proper regard to the replacement of the natural resources we employ.
As a publisher, we use a lot of wood pulp to make high-quality paper for printing, and that wood commonly comes
from spruce trees. We are therefore currently growing more than 500,000 trees in two Scottish forest plantations near
Aberdeen – Berrymoss (130 hectares/320 acres) and West Touxhill (125 hectares/305 acres). The forests we manage
contain twice the number of trees employed each year in paper-making for our books.
Because of this ongoing ecological investment programme, you, as our customer, can have the pleasure and
reassurance of knowing that a tree is being cultivated on your behalf to naturally replace the materials used
to make the book you are holding.
Our forestry programme is run in accordance with the UK Woodland Assurance Scheme (UKWAS) and will be
certified by the internationally recognized Forest Stewardship Council (FSC). The FSC is a non-government
organization dedicated to promoting responsible management of the world's forests. Certification ensures forests
are managed in an environmentally sustainable and socially responsible way. For further information about this
scheme, go to www.annesspublishing.com/trees

A CIP catalogue record for this book is available from the British Library.

Previously published as *Practical Handbook: Practical Home Paint Effects*

Contents

INTRODUCTION

R ecent years have seen a surge in interest in decorative paint effects. Perhaps as technology plays an increasing role in our lives we are eager to counteract its seeming impersonality by creating our own style and expressing our individuality more clearly in our homes.

This book features a wide variety of ideas that will enable you to make a decorative impact on the interior of your own home. There are inspirational decorating schemes using a variety of techniques, from simple colour treatments for the walls to fantasy decoration for furniture and accessories. All are described in easy-to-follow steps and lend themselves to easy adaptation according to your own creative ideas and skills.

ABOVE: An ordinary box is transformed with a dark wood effect. The black fern effect is painted freehand.

OPPOSITE: This Roman fresco of the 1st century AD from the House of Livia, Rome, features a dark green wall painted with garlands of flowers.

GETTING STARTED

The most important requirement for successful results in paint makeovers is the proper use of the correct materials and tools. With many of the techniques you can achieve stunning decoration with ordinary household paintbrushes, rollers, sponges and artist's brushes, but specialist equipment is needed for some effects. These items are available in decorators' suppliers and craft shops, where you can also ask for advice on their use.

Choose good quality materials. Make sure that you have the right type of paint suitable for the specific scheme you are planning. Read carefully through the steps to check that you have everything you need before you start.

ABOVE: A selection of pigments and stains that can be stirred into water-based paint mediums to create unique colours and textures.

OPPOSITE: You can get a different brush for just about every effect, but special brushes are not always necessary for the different techniques.

BASIC KIT

There are some basic essentials that you will need for decorating. You can add to this equipment gradually as you work on different effects.

- Use a sturdy set of steps to reach the tops of walls and ceilings easily.
- Buy a dust sheet (drop cloth) to protect the floor, furniture and anything precious. Cotton twill dust sheets (drop cloths) are reusable and preferable to the plastic-sheet disposable kind.
- You may sometimes have to remove door furniture or wall fixings, so both Phillips and flat-head screwdrivers are useful. They are also handy for removing paint can lids.
- For general painting, edging and painting woodwork, use household paintbrushes. The most useful sizes are 5cm/2in and 2.5cm/1in. Finer artist's brushes are invaluable for difficult small

spaces and touching up odd areas. Soft sable-haired artist's brushes with rounded edges are best for this use.
- Fill any chipped areas with interior filler (spackle or wood filler), applied with a filling knife, then sand to smooth
- It is sensible to use a paint kettle (pot). Pour the paint into the kettle (pot) a little at a time to make it lighter to hold. Also, in case of accident the spillage will not be so great.
- Use sandpaper to key and prepare previously painted woodwork. It is generally best used with a sanding block for a flatter finish.
- After sanding and prior to painting or staining, use a brush or cloth to dust away the sanded particles.

BELOW: Use a dust sheet to protect the floor from paint spots.

BRUSHES

Numerous types, sizes and qualities of brush are available for different techniques. Stencilling, for instance, is easier if you use a stencil brush, which has short, stiff bristles for stippling the paint. Also, the brush must hold the required quantity of paint, be the correct size for the surface area and made from the right type of hair. Natural hair and bristle brushes are best, but synthetic alternatives are less expensive and can give good results.

Clean your brushes well after use. If you are using oil-based paints and varnishes dip a third of the bristles in the paint and scrape off any excess. Do not leave a loaded brush for more than ten minutes or the paint will start to become tacky. First wipe the brush on to a rag, then rinse off as much of the paint as possible in white spirit (turpentine) or a non-toxic solvent. Scrape off any tough bits and wash the brush thoroughly in washing up liquid (dishwashing detergent) several times until clean. Rinse, shake off the water and reshape.

When using water-based paints or varnishes also make sure that the bristles are not totally covered. If there is a break in the work wash the brush immediately. Scrape off any excess paint, then rinse off under lukewarm water with a little detergent to remove strong colours. Shake off the water and reshape.

- Use a graining brush for certain wood grain effects. These are available in different sizes and with varying "pencils" or clumps of bristles.

- Softener (blending) brushes have soft bristles with rounded ends. Large ones are used for softening (blending) basic finishes and the first layers of faux effects. Smaller ones are used for delicate jobs and fine softening (blending). The best ones are made from badger hair, but are expensive. Use a large soft blusher brush as a good, cheap alternative.

- Dragging brushes are used for woodgraining and dragged effects. They are usually about 5cm/2in or 7.5cm/3in wide. A household brush can be used as an alternative.

- Household paintbrushes are available in a wide variety of sizes. The bristle quality and length tends to vary, and it is best to choose longer bristles. These brushes are used for all basic painting, edging and varnishing.

- Stippling brushes have large blocks of short-cut bristles attached to an angled handle. They are used for stippling, that is, making fine pin-point marks. Stippling brushes are available in various sizes. You can use a masonry brush as an alternative.

- Liner brushes are long, soft brushes used for lining, and for marbling effects. A swordliner (above) is an angled version. Different sizes are available.

ROLLERS AND SPONGES

Many types of specialist rollers are used in decorating. Specific covers are suitable for different surfaces and you can buy rollers designed for particular patterns. A radiator roller is similar, with a long handle for reaching into tight spots. Use much smaller craft and mini-rollers for applying paint in techniques such as stamping. Paint pads (pad painters) can also be useful for clean, flat painting and precise edges and are made from plastic foam, with a short-haired pile inserted into an applicator or handle.

A selection of natural and synthetic sponges is essential for numerous overall decorating techniques, as are lint-free cloths and rags. Each makes its own individual marks, so experiment with the effects.

- Mini-rollers have a cover made from dense foam or pile. Available in several widths, they are used for painting narrow stripes or coating stamps.

- Masonry rollers are generally 23cm/9in wide with a long pile. Use for covering rough surfaces and for roller fidgeting.
- Sheepskin rollers are used for basic quick coverage of flat paint. They are usually available in 18cm/7in and 23cm/9in widths.
- Use a sponge roller as a cheaper alternative to a sheepskin one. Sponge rollers are also available in 18cm/7in and 23cm/9in widths.
- Natural sponges are mostly used for sponging. Synthetic sponges make a more obvious mark than natural sponges, so use natural ones for tight, fine marks and for marbling.
- A chamois, made from real leather, can be scrunched into a ball for ragging. Or use a special ragging chamois, made from strips bound together.

BELOW: Clockwise from top left; natural sponge, cloth, pinched-out sponge, synthetic sponge, two paint pads, mini-roller, small cellulose sponge, gloss roller, masonry roller, ragging chamois.

RIGHT: Clockwise from top left; spirit level, long ruler, sanding block, two combs, plumb line, tape measure, heart grainer (graining roller), sanding sponge, craft knife, pencil, selection of sand paper (far right).

BELOW: A triangular comb and a graduated comb.

SPECIALIST TOOLS

There are many items that will make it easier to plan your decoration. For careful measuring and marking before you start, you may need a spirit level (level), long ruler, tape measure and pencil. A plumb line, which consists of a small weight suspended on a fine string, is helpful for marking vertical drops. Masking tape is useful for keeping edges straight and covering light switches and sockets.

For specialist techniques certain tools are needed. Different shapes of rubber combs will give a variety of woodgrain effects. A heart grainer (graining roller) with its moulded surface will enable you to reproduce the characteristics of a particular wood more accurately. For gilding, a gilder's pad is a useful investment and consists of a soft pad surrounded by a screen of parchment to shield gild leaf from draughts. Craft knives can be bought with double-ended blades that

ABOVE: This lighter-weight craft knife has a retractable blade. When it becomes blunt, simply snap off the end for a new edge.

are screwed into the handle and turned or replaced when blunt. Others have a long retractable strip blade that allows you to break off and dispose of the blunt portion. For safety, keep your fingers behind the cutting edge. Never leave the knife within reach of children or where it will be a danger to animals; a cork is a good "lid" to put on the end of the blade. Use craft knives for cutting stencils and stamps.

Keep a supply of different grades of sandpaper, and a sanding block to use with them. An electric (power) sander can also save time on larger jobs. For floorboards a special industrial sander should be hired.

PAINTS

Different paints are suitable for different surfaces and effects and it is important to choose the right paint for the right surface. The projects in this book suggest the easiest and most effective type to use for each particular effect.

Traditional paints are either water-based or oil-based and generally come in three finishes – matt (flat), satin (mid sheen) and gloss. Most basic wall effects are painted with water-based emulsion (latex) paint since it is easy to apply with a variety of brushes, rollers, sponges and rags. It makes a good base coat, mixes well and several layers can be painted over each other to build up the desired effect. You can tint water-based emulsions (latex) paints with acrylic paints to make your own colours.

Artists' oil colours are frequently used for faux effects. The rich pigments replicate the colours found in different types of wood, marble and other natural surfaces. Oil paints take longer to dry than water-based paints and this can be an advantage if you need to take time in creating a precise effect. They give a more durable finish, but they are a little harder to work with. For a realistic result use enamel paints for metal effects.

Many surfaces benefit from the application of a primer. Primer paints seal and provide a suitable base for paint finishes. They are particularly important if you are working on a porous surface and essential for bare wood. Read the information on the can to make sure you are choosing the correct primer for the specific surface. An undercoat on top of a primer protects the surface further and helps to give a smooth base for the top coat. Oil-based undercoats tend to be used most frequently for painting woodwork.

BELOW: Traditional household paints are available in a tempting array of luscious colours.

HOUSEHOLD PAINTS

These are available in a wide range of finishes from completely matt through varying sheens to high glosses. There is a wealth of colour choice and in many DIY (do-it-yourself) stores you can have an exact colour matched and specially mixed for you. Read the instructions on the can before use to check that it is suitable for your surface. When thinning paint make sure that you are using the correct diluent.

Household paints	Base	Diluent	Uses	Notes
Matt emulsion (latex)	water	water, wallpaper paste acrylic glaze, acrylic varnish, clean with water	basic walls, large choice of colours, flat finish	fast drying, needs varnishing on furniture, marks easily
Silk emulsion (latex)	water	as above	as above faint sheen	fast drying, more hard-wearing than matt, needs varnishing on furniture
Soft sheen	water	as above	kitchens and bathrooms, mid sheen	fast drying, moisture resistant, needs varnishing on furniture
Dead flat oil	oil	linseed oil, white spirit (turpentine), oil glaze, oil varnishes	woodwork, flat/velvet finish	marks easily, not durable
Eggshell	oil	as above	woodwork, faint sheen, furniture	more resistant than above, but still marks
Satin	oil	as above	woodwork, mid sheen, furniture	durable, washable finish
Gloss	oil	as above	woodwork, high sheen, exterior furniture	tough, hard-wearing finish, washable
Primer	oil	not to be diluted, clean with spirits (alcohol)	bare wood	necessary for porous or wood surfaces
Undercoat	oil	not to be diluted, clean with spirits (alcohol)	between the primer and top coat	saves on top coats, choose the right colour
Masonry	water	not to be diluted, clean with water	exterior masonry	limited colours, apply with a suitable roller
Floor	oil	not to be diluted, clean with spirits (alcohol)	floors, light or industrial use	tough, durable, apply with a roller

MODERN PAINTS

Major advances in paint technology have widened the creative possibilities for the home decorator and there is a constant stream of new paints to try. The invention and manufacture of synthetic pigments have resulted in paints that are more permanent in colour and give predictable results. Developments in paint composition have produced modern paints that are easy to apply, cover well and dry quickly. As well as being available in cans they come in many different convenient forms, such as spray aerosols, as a solid block for use with rollers, and in non-drip and one-coat formulas.

Many of the techniques for basic broken-colour and patterned effects can be adapted for use on surfaces other than walls and wood. There are now many specialist paints designed for different purposes and materials, such as glass, fabrics and metals. These paints sometimes need to be handled slightly differently from conventional household paints, but experimenting with them is well worth the effort. Stencil paints are designed specifically to use with stencils and come in useful small pots or oil-based stencil sticks, which are easy for blending.

Acrylic and enamel paints have numerous uses. Acrylic paints are water-based, and can be added to other water-based paints or used on their own to paint decorative motifs and flourishes. Enamel paints are oil based, and are suitable for metal and other surfaces that require a particularly tough finish. Both acrylic and enamel paints dry to a durable, washable finish and are available in a massive range of colours, including metallic finishes.

BELOW: A selection of different-coloured paints, including watercolours, stencil paints and acrylics.

TRADITIONAL PAINTS

With the current vogue for restoring old buildings there is renewed enthusiasm for traditional paints made from natural ingredients. Many decorative techniques are designed to give an aged effect and the mellow colours and soft appearance of these paints are ideal. Many of them are earth colours, but they also include some surprisingly bright colours without the more garish characteristics of many modern paints. These are suitable for distressed techniques and antiquing.

Traditional paints are made with natural additives that give a particular finish. Powdered pigments can be used to colour paint, while chalk gives a powdery surface. Use gesso, a white powder prepared with rabbit skin glue, to make a smooth painting surface. Scumble glaze is a transparent medium, made from linseed and other oils, whiting and dryers, which can be used with colour pigments to make various thicknesses of tinted glazes. Milk paints were originally made with milk derivatives and give a dense, matt surface.

RIGHT: This palette of traditional folk paints shows the variety of hues that can be made from natural pigments.

Traditional paints	Base	Diluent	Uses	Notes
Milk paints	water	water wallpaper paste	basic wall large surface areas	dense, matt surface
Distemper (tempera)	powder	water and glue size	woodwork furniture	good for antique effects
Chalk	water	as above	as above	powdery surface
Limewash	water	as above	as above	good for aged effect
Gesso	powder	rabbit skin glue	layered for a smooth finish before gilding or marbling	labour intensive
Powder paint	powder	any	tints anything	can be gritty
Gilt cream	oil	oil varnishes white spirit (turpentine)	easy gilding techniques	metallic colours

BINDERS AND DILUENTS

Pigment needs a binder so that it will adhere to the surface on which it is painted. As well as the binder in the manufacture of the paint there are other binders that you can add to modify its consistency and texture. Diluents and solvents are added to thin the paint and to delay the drying time. Glazes also delay drying and modern products such as acrylic glazes can be used instead of traditional scumble glazes for an easier consistency.

There are many mediums for glazes such as wallpaper paste, linseed oil, PVA (white glue) and dryers that will change the nature of the paint. Solvents such as white spirit can also be used to clean paintbrushes. Make sure you use a diluent or solvent that is suitable for the type of paint you are using.

RIGHT: *A selection of glues and solvents, including wood glue, PVA (white glue), spray adhesive and rubber solution.*

Binders and Diluents	Base	Diluent	Uses	Notes
PVA	water	water	binder for emulsion (latex) washes	makes the mixture more durable
White spirit	oil		paint thinner, brush cleaner	buy in bulk
Linseed oil	oil		medium for powder	lengthy drying
Dryers			add to oil paint to speed drying	
Wallpaper paste	water	water	dilutes emulsions (latex)	retards the drying a little
Acrylic glaze	water	water	as above	retards drying
Scumble glaze	oil	white spirit (turpentine)	medium to suspend colour pigments	difficult to tint to the right quantity
Methylated spirits (methyl alcohol)	oil		softens dried emulsion	
White spirit (Turpentine)	oil		paint thinner, brush cleaner	

Varnishes	Base	Diluent	Uses	Notes
Polyurethane/oil-based	oil	white spirit (turpentine)	strong varnishes in a range of finishes	tough, durable, slow drying
Polyurethane (aerosol)	oil		flat finish	
Acrylic	water	water	range of finishes	not as durable
Acrylic (aerosol)	water		flat finish	
Tinted varnish	oil acrylic	white spirit (turpentine) water	for bare wood, or antiquing paint. Range of colours	slow drying fast drying
Crackle glaze	water	not to be diluted	medium which makes a top coat crackle over a contrasting base coat	reliability of brands varies
Japan gold size	oil	not to be diluted	adhesive medium for gold leaf	quickest drying of the range
Button polish (shellac)	water	methylated spirits	sealing bare wood	quick drying

VARNISHES

Varnishes seal and protect the surface of the paint, preserving your decoration. There are specific formulas for interior or exterior use and they are usually available in matt (flat), satin (mid sheen) or gloss finishes. Modern varnishes have been developed with a polyurethane or acrylic base. Special mediums such as crackle glaze can be used to produce a cracked protective surface, ideal for an antiqued or distressed effect. Size acts as a sealant and as a base for gilding.

Varnishes are bought in liquid form or as aerosol sprays. Gloss varnish produces a shiny finish, while matt varnish has a flat look. Make sure the varnish you buy is appropriate for interior or exterior use. There are several types of crackle medium on the market, so read the manufacturer's instructions carefully before using one. There are also modern fast-drying or traditional forms of gold size.

Bronze powders are available in several metallic finishes and are used over gold size. You can also use Dutch leaf, which is a less expensive substitute for real gold leaf and gives a good result.

RIGHT: Pots of varnish on a crackle glaze background.

PAINT REMOVAL

Over several years and many applications of paint there can be quite a build-up of layers on a surface. This is not really a problem on walls and ceilings, but on woodwork and metalwork it is a different matter. Attractive mouldings, especially on skirting (base) boards, window frames and architraves, can become clogged and their features indistinct. In addition, moving parts on doors and windows, such as hinges, and the edges of the frames can start to become ill fitting. The answer to this is to strip off the old paint right back to the wood or metal.

Stripping is also the best option if the paintwork looks in poor condition. It may be deeply chipped or have been badly painted, leaving drips and blobs on the surface. In these cases it is unlikely that a new coat of paint will disguise the imperfections on the surface.

You can remove thick layers of old paint with a chemical paint remover in the form of a paste or a liquid stripper that you brush over the paint surface. Wait for the chemicals to react with the paint, then scrape it off with a paint scraper. These chemicals are strong, so read the manufacturer's instructions carefully before applying them and use them properly.

Another way to strip off old paint is to use an electric heat gun. Again, keep safety well in mind and

ABOVE: The chipped paint on this old chair can easily be removed using one of the techniques shown, and then transformed with a new paint effect.

wear safety glasses or goggles to protect your eyes. Too much heat can scorch the wood or crack glass if you are not careful. Put the old scrapings in a metal container as you work and cover surrounding areas such as the floor to protect them.

Using liquid stripper

1 Carefully pour some of the stripper into an old glass jar. Then, wearing rubber gloves to protect your hands, brush the stripper on to the painted surface. Leave it until the paint starts to bubble, following the manufacturer's instructions.

2 Scrape off the peeling layers of paint with a paint scraper. Use a shavehook for intricate mouldings.

3 Wash the surface with water or white spirit (turpentine), as recommended by the manufacturer. This will neutralize the chemicals. Then leave to dry.

Using a heat gun

1 Move the heat gun over the surface so that the air stream heats and softens the paint evenly. Scrape off the paint as you work.

2 Be careful not to scorch the wood, especially when working on intricate areas such as mouldings. Use a shavehook to scrape out the paint from these areas.

3 Wearing rubber gloves to protect your hands, rub off any remaining bits of paint with wire (steel) wool soaked in white spirit (turpentine). Work in the direction of the grain of the wood.

4 Clean any particles of paint out of the crevices in the mouldings with a hand vacuum cleaner.

5 Lightly sand the surface of the wood to smooth it. Wipe any dust away with a clean cloth dampened with a little white spirit (turpentine) or a tack cloth.

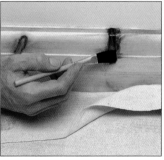

6 Finally, seal any knots in the wood so that the resin cannot escape. Do this by brushing on liquid knotting or shellac. Leave to dry.

Using paste remover

1 These strippers dry slowly and are ideal for stripping intricate mouldings. Wear rubber gloves to protect your hands and apply a thick coating of paste remover to the woodwork.

2 Leave the paste to work, following the manufacturer's instructions. Thick layers of paint will need more time. Use a paint scraper to scrape off the paint. Then wash the surface well with water.

SURFACE PREPARATION

Perhaps the most important factor in achieving a successful result in decorating is to make sure that the surfaces are clean and smooth. Careful preparation can seem rather tedious but it is worth the time spent.

Wash walls with a solution of sugar soap, then rinse them well with clean water. Scrape off any pieces of flaking paint and fix any dents and cracks in the plaster with filler (spackle) and a filler knife. When the filler (spackle) has hardened, sand it smooth with fine-grade sandpaper. Similarly, fix any defects in the woodwork. If knots are showing through the existing paintwork, sand them back and apply knotting or shellac. When dry, paint on primer and undercoat to bring the area level with the rest of the surface of the woodwork.

Clean surfaces such as ceramic tiles, china or glass with soapy water and dry them well with a lint-free cloth. You will then need to use specialist paints, as emulsion (latex) and acrylic paints will not adhere well to these smooth surfaces.

Preparing woodwork

1 Sand down the surface with fine-grade sandpaper over a sanding block. This smoothes the surface of old bits of paint and provides a key to which the new paint can adhere.

2 Wash the paintwork with water and detergent to make sure that it is completely clean of grease and dust. Then rinse it well with clean water so that there is no detergent left to prevent the new paint from adhering.

3 Dampen a clean cloth with white spirit (turpentine) or a tack cloth to remove any dust from intricate mouldings and corners.

Filling defects in woodwork

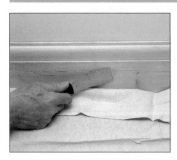  

1 With a putty knife, stop any holes, dents or cracks in the wood. Use ordinary filler (spackle) for wood that will be painted, and tinted wood filler for wood that will be varnished.

2 Work the filler into corners with your finger or the corner of a putty knife. Smooth off any excess or edges before the filler dries.

3 When the filler is hard, sand it down so that it is flush with the surface of the wood. The best way to do this is by using fine-grade sandpaper wrapped around a sanding block.

Preparing shiny surfaces

1 Wash shiny surfaces such as tile, china or glass with soapy water. Then rinse them well.

2 Wipe them with a clean cloth dampened with methylated spirits to make sure no grease remains.

Filling cracks in plaster

1 Rake out loose material from the crack with the corner of a putty knife. Undercut the edges of the crack slightly to provide an edge to which the filler (spackle) can grip.

2 Use an old paintbrush to brush out any debris and dust. You could also use the crevice fitment of a vacuum cleaner for this job.

3 Use a water spray to dampen the plaster around the crack so that the filler will not dry too quickly and cause further cracks.

4 Mix up some powdered filler (spackle) on a board, following the manufacturer's instructions. Or use ready-mixed filler if you prefer.

5 Press the filler into the crack with a filling knife. Draw the blade of the knife across the filled crack and then along it. The filler should stand slightly proud of the surrounding surface.

6 When the filler is completely hard sand it smooth so that it is level with the surrounding surface. Do this with a piece of fine-grade sandpaper wrapped around a sanding block.

USING BRUSHES AND ROLLERS

Paint is applied using brushes, rollers or paint pads (pad painters). Brushes are available in a range of widths, so choose one that is suitable for the surface you are painting – for instance, use a narrow brush for the glazing bars of a window. For large areas use a wide brush, or a roller for fast coverage.

If you wish to paint with a previously used brush that has not been kept covered, wash it well first to remove any bits and pieces. Leave it to dry before using it. Check that the ferrule of the brush is securely fixed to the handle and clean off any traces of rust with wire (steel) wool or sandpaper.

Rollers are excellent for large flat areas. Choose a suitable sleeve depending on whether you are painting on smooth plaster or a textured surface. You may also need to use a brush in corners where the roller will not fit. Paint pads (pad painters) cover less quickly than brushes or rollers, but they apply paint more smoothly.

Preparing the paint

1 Wipe the lid of the can first to get rid of any dust. Prise the lid off gently with a wide lever so that you do not damage the lip.

2 Pour some paint into a clean paint kettle (pot) or bucket. You will find a container with a handle easier to work with and replacing the lid on the can will keep the rest of the paint fresher.

3 Use up old paint by first removing any skin from the top, then straining it through a clean piece of cheesecloth (muslin) or an old, fine silk stocking.

Using a brush

1 When using a new brush for the first time remove any stray hairs by working it vigorously across the palm of your hand.

2 Use small or medium brushes by placing your fingers on one side of the ferrule and your thumb on the other. This gives you better control.

3 Hold wide brushes by the handle or your hand will quickly become tired.

Using a roller

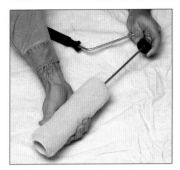

1 Choose a sleeve with a suitable pile and place on the sprung metal cage.

2 Pour the paint into a roller tray until it just overlaps the deeper part.

3 Paint a band in the corners and angles where the roller will not fit.

4 Load the roller by rolling it down the slope of the tray into the paint.

5 Apply the paint by using the roller in overlapping diagonal movements.

6 Blend the sections together by working in parallel to the edges.

Applying the paint

1 Dip only a third of the bristles into the paint. If you put too much paint on the brush you will cause paint to run down the handle or make drips.

2 Tie a piece of wire or string across the top of the paint kettle (pot) or bucket so that you can scrape off excess paint against it.

3 Use long sweeping strokes to apply the paint, working in the direction of the grain, until the paint on the brush is used. Then reload with paint and apply it to the next section.

4 Blend the two sections together with short, light strokes. Paint edges and corners by letting the brush run off the edge and repeating the process on the opposite edge.

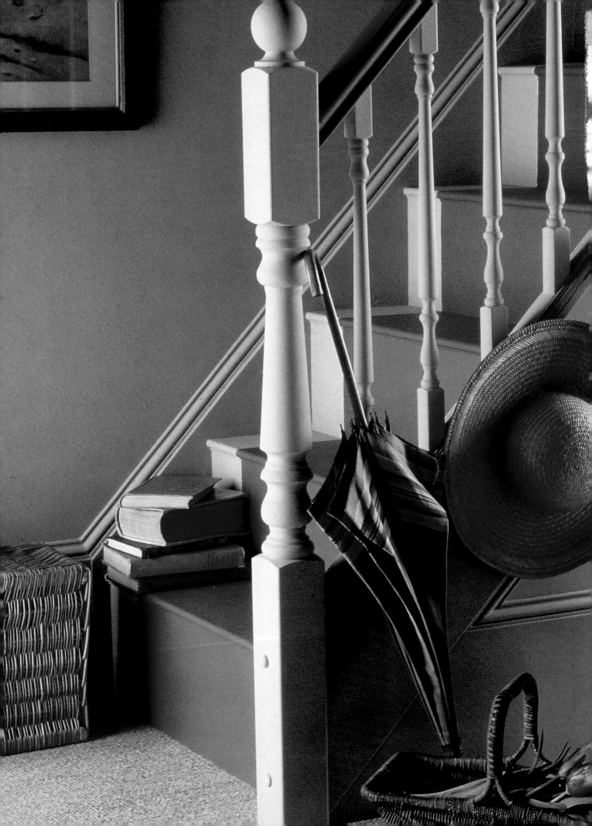

USING COLOUR

Colour can have tremendous impact in our homes. The colours we choose for our surroundings reflect our personalities, lifestyles, travels and interests. They set the scene for an atmosphere of relaxation or stimulation, for quiet contemplation or family get-togethers and parties.

We live in a world that contains millions of natural colours. Today, using synthetic dyes and stainers, we can match almost any colour found in nature in the form of paint, fabrics and other materials. An understanding of the visual effects that these different colours can produce will help you plan creative and successful decorating schemes.

ABOVE: For special effects watercolour, acrylic and special stencil paints are invaluable. The colour palette is more restricted than with household paints, but you can have great fun mixing your own shades.

OPPOSITE: The coolness or vibrancy of a colour has a major effect on the appearance of a room. Here, pale blue walls are prevented from looking cold by being teamed with warm yellow and orange colours.

COLOUR TERMINOLOGY

Knowing some of the generally accepted theories of how colour works will enable you to use colours to their best advantage and for particular purposes. Artists, designers and decorators use precise terms to describe colours and the differences between them.

Red, yellow and blue are known as primary colours. These are colours that cannot be produced from a combination of other pigments. Mixing two primary colours produces the secondary colours: red and yellow results in orange, yellow and blue in green, and blue and red in violet.

Placing primary and secondary colours in a circle in their appropriate positions forms a colour wheel. Tertiary colours can then be produced by mixing a primary colour with a secondary colour that is next to it. For instance, red mixed with violet gives red-violet. Experiment by making your own colour wheel, mixing adjacent colours for an infinite variety.

ABOVE: Colours that are immediately opposite each other on the colour wheel are termed complementary. For example, violet is complementary to yellow, and green to red. These opposites enhance each other and make each appear more intense. Here green is painted next to a tint of its complementary red (pink). The colours really seem to glow against each other.

BELOW: Tints are made by adding white to a colour, and shades by adding black. These pastel stripes show tints of colours. They are all also similar in tone - they have the same amount of light or dark.

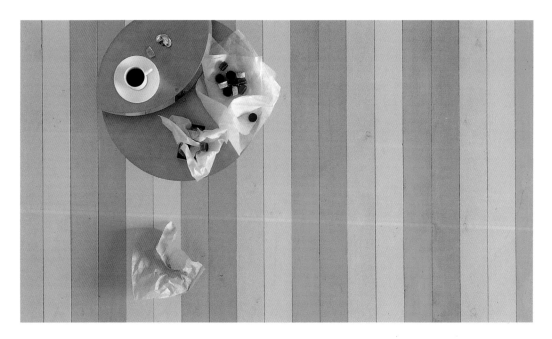

ABOVE: *Colours that are near each other on the colour wheel are called harmonious. Having elements in common, they relate and work well together. For instance, the swatches of main colour shown here work well with the dashes of colour painted below them.*

BELOW: *Contrasting colours can also give a dramatic effect. These are colours that are not related at all, but create impact because they are of the same tone. The main colour swatches shown here are matched in intensity by the dashes of colour painted below them.*

DENSITY OF COLOUR

The amount of colour used in a room and where it is placed can create a dramatic or a subtle effect. Use it in large areas to create an overall atmosphere or in selected small areas to emphasize particular features. Clever use of colour can appear to change the proportions of a room, making it appear bigger or smaller than it really is. Remember that your furniture and fabrics are all part of the same scheme. Be careful not to use too many colours or the effect will be unbalanced.

LEFT: The more intense a colour is, the more we notice it. Adding a gloss finish or glazing surfaces can make them look much brighter. This chair is varnished, making it stand out as well as protecting the distressed paint effect.

BELOW: It is generally accepted that colours towards the red end of the spectrum appear to advance. However, an intense red used in a large area can look overpowering. Here, a dramatic effect is produced by using areas of different reds, allowing the eye to move constantly forwards and backwards.

ABOVE: Towards the other end of the spectrum from red, blue is a colour that seems to recede. It is therefore useful to use in decorating schemes where you want to increase the feeling of space. Here intense blue and yellow accessories balance each other visually on the sill, but the pale blue shutters beyond lead the eye out of the window, making the room seem bigger.

COLOUR AND LIGHT

When you are choosing paints or coloured materials for your home make sure that you look at the colours in natural daylight at different times of the day. A colour in a room facing the sun varies from morning to night, while a colour in a room that does not receive much, if any, direct sunlight remains largely consistent. Colours can look quite different in artificial light too.

Seasons and geographical location also have an influence on our impressions of colour. A bright colour that you see on vacation under a glaring Caribbean sun may not work as well in your own living room, but you may be able to modify it. You can also tone colours down by adding a little of the complementary colour.

RIGHT: This Indian-style room is decorated with just two bright primary colours – red and yellow. However, the jewel-like scarlet is balanced by the natural ochre colour so that the effect is rich and warm rather than garish. The sheen finish on the walls reflects the light in the room and the sheer curtain fabric gently diffuses light coming through the window.

COLOUR AND TEXTURE

Textures can emphasize the general effect given by colour. We associate hard, glossy finishes with streamlining and efficiency and so they tend to look cold, especially when used with colours in the blue range. Warm-looking traditional surfaces such as soft, grainy woods and rich, textured fabrics that suggest age and reliability enhance the effect of reds, oranges and browns. General paint effects such as combing and rag rolling can be lightly or heavily textured, so when you are choosing colours think carefully about the overall effect you want to create.

RIGHT: *Colour and texture combine here to produce a restful environment, yet one full of visual interest. The walls have been dry-brushed in green and purple – two shades that always work well together – creating an illusion of texture, while the grapevine border was made using a bought stencil.*

BELOW: *Everything in this room speaks of warmth and comfort. The faux-effect wood panelling sets the scene, and the soft, grained effect is enhanced by the cream walls. Furniture with traditional coverings such as leather and rush are timeless and lend an air of comfort.*

NATURAL SHADES

The colours and textures of nature can be brought into home decoration and used over and over again to add a calming note. They are surfaces that are always interesting and diverse, yet complement any environment and style, old or new, classic or modern. The shades you choose may be bright or subtle.

Greens and blues are perennial favourites in home decoration, either used singly in toning shades or together. Browns, soft oranges, buttermilk yellows, beiges and creams are also natural colours that harmonize well in the home; they are often seen in country-style kitchens, reinforcing the sense of warmth and comfort. Neutral colour schemes allow you to use a mixture of textures for visual variety. They can also act as a foil to small areas of bright colours that can be changed from time to time to give a different accent to a room.

RIGHT: These pale greens and blues in a matt (flat) finish suggest the places in which we find escape in the heat of summer, such as cool water or shady areas. The walls are defined by clean white lines of matt skirting (base) board, and the wood-washed floor looks as if it has faded in the sun.

RIGHT: This entire scheme relies on a neutral palette of off-white, accessorized with metal furniture and gold-accented ornaments. The wall motifs were created using a stamp dipped in a mixture of stone white and interior filler (spackle) and add subtle highlights and texture to the wall.

DECORATING
SCHEMES

The most exciting part about using paint effects is planning how they will work together. You may want to decorate a room with a particular theme, or combine specific effects with distinctive colours. The following pages suggest all the factors to consider, and give some ideas for decorating schemes based on colour, patterns and styles from around the world. You can follow the steps for the projects exactly or use elements from them, adapting them to your own taste. Most describe a basic treatment for the walls and show some simple finishes for added decoration.

ABOVE: *A flag motif stamped on to the wall of this kitchen instantly gives the room a nautical feel.*

OPPOSITE: *The pattern on the walls perfectly complements the Scandinavian theme of this living room.*

CHOOSING A SCHEME

Before dashing straight for the colour cards and paint pots take time to think exactly what you want to achieve when you decorate your home. You need to consider if the scheme you are choosing will succeed in the room you wish to paint.

Take a good look at the room. Take into account the size and how much light it receives. This can make the difference between a room that receives almost no direct sunlight and one that will be sunny and bright for much of the day. If east or west facing it may receive sunlight only in the morning or afternoon. Light can radically change the appearance of colours. The shape of the room can also have some bearing, as light may be angled more strongly in some areas depending on the position of the windows, doors and alcoves. Make sure you see the colours in the actual room at different times of the day.

Look at the colours that are already in the room. There may be much that you cannot change, such as

furniture, carpets and curtains, and you will have to plan your colours and effects around these. Figure out your scheme with these fixed items in mind.

Choose colours and effects for the atmosphere that you want to create – warm and cosy or cool and spacious. They can also be used to give the visual impression of changing the shape of a room. Warm colours seem to advance, so use these if you want to make a room look smaller. Cool colours recede and are

OPPOSITE: The light colours used in this scheme give the kitchen a suitably fresh and airy feel.

BELOW: A wall decoration could be influenced by the soft colours, textures and shapes of a collection of ceramics.

BELOW LEFT: A frottage effect above dado height teams perfectly with wallpaper below. The soft green colour is a restful shade to choose for any room, including a narrow hallway.

useful for making a room look bigger. Similarly, dark tones tend to advance and light tones recede, so use shades of colour to visually move space. For instance, if you have a high ceiling that you wish to appear lower, paint the walls in a dark colour to picture rail height, then white above this and over the ceiling to reduce the wall height. You can also emphasize certain elements in the room in this way.

Patterns can be used to change space, too. Large, bold-coloured motifs tend to attract the eye, so use them in areas that you wish to bring forward. Small muted patterns tend to merge into an overall textured effect unless you are close to them. Vertical patterns such as stripes will give the impression of heightening an area, while horizontal ones will widen it. Remember that texture will also have some effect by breaking up the surface and disguising imperfections.

Bear in mind the age of the building you are decorating. Consider whether a particular style or theme is appropriate to the architecture. There may be existing original features that you can plan a theme around. Perhaps you can adapt elements in the design of the furniture or fittings to create a completely original theme. A motif from the design of the curtains, for instance, can be used as a basis for a stencil or stamp pattern. The overall style of the room could be

ABOVE: Trompe d'oeil *china plates painted over antiqued shelves immediately suggest a country home interior.*

BELOW: *A hand-painted and stamped frieze adds colour and decoration to a child's room. Here the frieze is just part of the overall design with the green skirting (base) board standing in for grass and the walls decorated with a sky effect.*

ABOVE: A stamped rose motif on a neutral background is quick and simple to do. The motif has been used again to decorate a cream-upholstered director's chair to pull the scheme together.

enhanced with faux effects such as verdigris candlesticks, pewter vases or copper plates. Let your imagination run wild.

Flick through magazines and books, find a colour scheme that appeals and see how you can interpret it into your own interior. Try out your ideas on paper – even a rough sketch with the colours and the main elements of the room in place will help you see whether the scheme will work. Use paint samples so that you are accurate in your choice of colour. The more care you take in planning, the more successful the result is likely to be.

The amount of time and money you have available for decorating are important considerations. If you have only limited time, choose an effect that you will be able to complete without leaving the job half done. Practise the paint techniques before starting on a large-scale project for a room. Check that the type of paint you are going to use is suitable for the particular technique you have chosen. Also figure out how much paint and other materials you will need so that the cost for completing the whole scheme falls within your budget.

Another important point to remember is paint safety. Make sure you have all the equipment you need before you start. Take great care when using stepladders. Make sure they are safe before climbing them. Do not lean out in an effort to paint an odd corner, but get down and move the ladder nearer to the place you want to paint. Keep paints and solvents well out of the way of children and animals. Store solvents and thinners tightly capped in their original containers with the relevant labels intact. Put them in a dark, cool area away from heat.

Finally, have fun with your decorating scheme. With careful planning and a bit of practice you will find that not only do you have a new skill, but you can change the interior of your house with the stroke of a brush.

SCANDINAVIAN LIVING ROOM

Create a cool atmosphere with this sophisticated Gustavian-influenced wall stamping. This project requires some preparatory work, but the elegance of the result justifies the little extra time. The stamps are cut from high-density foam or foam rubber which can be mounted on blocks of composition (mat) board with a small drawer knob added for easy handling, if required. Before you do any stamping, draw a grid down the wall using a plumb line and a cardboard square. If you find the effect of the two blues too cool, you can add warmth by applying a coat of tinted varnish to the wall, ageing the whole effect.

You will need

- wood glue
- 2 pieces of composition (mat) board, 9cm x 9cm/3^1/$_2$in x 3^1/$_2$in
- 2 pieces of high-density foam rubber, such as upholstery foam, 9cm x 9cm/3^1/$_2$in x 3^1/$_2$in
- tracing paper
- pencil
- spray adhesive
- craft knife
- ruler
- 2 small wooden drawer knobs
- plumb line
- cardboard 18cm x 18cm/7in x 7in
- plate
- emulsion (latex) paint in dark blue
- square-tipped paintbrush

1 Apply wood glue to the composition (mat) board squares and stick the foam rubber on to them. Leave to dry.

2 Trace and transfer the shapes from the back of the book. Spray with adhesive and place on the foam rubber.

3 Cut around the edges of the designs and remove the paper pattern. Scoop out the background to leave the stamp free of the composition (mat) board.

4 Draw two intersecting lines across the back of the composition (mat) board and glue a wooden drawer knob in the centre to finish the stamp.

5 Attach a plumb line at ceiling height to give a vertical guideline (this can be done with a piece of masking tape) on the wall. Mark a point 8cm/3¼in above the dado (chair) rail and place one corner of the cardboard square on it, lined up along the plumb line. Mark all the corners of the cardboard square on the wall in pencil, then move it up, continuing to mark the corners. Use this system to mark a grid of squares across the whole surface of the upper wall.

6 One of the stamps has a static motif and the other has a swirl. Use the static one first, dipping it into a plate coated with paint and making the first print on a sheet of scrap paper to make sure that the stamp is not overloaded. Then print up the wall, from the 8cm/3¼in mark.

7 Continue printing, working in a diagonal up the wall.

8 Change to the swirl motif, and stamp this pattern in the spaces between the static motifs.

9 Use a pencil and ruler to draw a line 3.5cm/1½in above the level of the dado (chair) rail, all the way along the stamped section of wall.

10 Fill the space between the pencil line and the dado (chair) rail with diluted dark blue emulsion paint, using a square-tipped paintbrush.

RIGHT: The flat blue wall with its stamp motif creates a dynamic background for the elegant mirrors and the delicate wooden furniture.

PENNSYLVANIA DUTCH TULIPS

This American folk art inspired idea uses the rich colours and simple motifs inspired by nature and beloved by the German and Dutch immigrants to Pennsylvania. Create the effect of all-over hand-painted wallpaper in a hallway or living room using two different stencil shapes or, for a beginner's project, take a single motif and use it to decorate a key cupboard, a chest of drawers or perhaps the top of a wooden chest.

You will need

- emulsion (latex) paint in dark ochre
- large and small paintbrushes
- woodwash (wood stain) in indigo blue and mulberry
- tracing paper
- stencil card (card stock)
- craft knife and cutting mat
- pencil
- ruler
- masking tape
- stencil brushes
- stencil paints in red, light green, dark green and pale brown
- saucer or cloth
- fine artist's brush

1 Dilute one part ochre emulsion (latex) with one part water. Using a large paintbrush, cover the top half of the wall with the diluted emulsion (latex). Use vertical brush strokes for an even texture.

2 Paint the lower half of the wall underneath the dado (chair) rail with indigo blue woodwash (wood stain). Finish the surface with a curving line using a dry brush to suggest woodgrain.

3 Paint the dado (chair) rail or a strip at dado-rail height in mulberry woodwash (wood stain) using a narrow brush to give a clean edge.

4 Trace the tulip template from the back of the book and make your own heart template to match. Cut the stencils from stencil card (card stock). Mark the centre of each edge of the stencil. Measure the wall and divide it into equal sections, so that the repeats will fall at about 20cm/8in intervals. Mark the positions lightly with pencil, so that they can be erased later.

5 Dip the stencil brush into red stencil paint. Rub the brush on a saucer or cloth until it is almost dry before stencilling in the tulips. Leave to dry.

6 Paint the leaves in light green stencil paint with darker green shading. Paint the stems in dark green using an artist's brush. Leave to dry.

7 Stencil the tulip basket in pale brown stencil paint using a chunky stencil brush to apply the paint.

8 Stencil a single heart between each two baskets of tulips using red stencil paint and a chunky brush.

9 Decorate a matching key cupboard following the same method and using just one motif in the centre.

RIGHT: These bright country colours will instantly lift a dull hallway, bringing a touch of spring into your home with the use of a charming floral theme.

TARTAN (PLAID) STUDY

A warm-looking and well-ordered study is an encouragement to settle down to some writing, reading or serious contemplation! Time-honoured plaids exude a feeling of comforting reliability and a tartan border is much less complicated to paint than you might think. Again, careful measuring is the secret to success and you can use this technique to design any number of combinations of colours and checks. Antique office furniture is expensive, but it is a simple matter to paint an inexpensive desk with a dark wood effect and an attractive leather inset.

1 Apply two coats of claret red emulsion (latex) paint to the walls that you wish to decorate. Leave to dry.

2 Decide how wide and deep you wish the tartan (plaid) border to be. Then measure and mark it out with a pencil. Taking into account the widths of the roller, mask off the horizontal edges with low-tack masking tape.

3 Measure and mark out a grid for the main check by drawing in the vertical lines, again taking into account the width of roller you will be using.

4 Coat the mini roller with dark green emulsion (latex) paint and pull along the horizontal pencil lines. Leave to dry.

5 Add the vertical lines in dark green using the mini roller.

6 Dilute gold acrylic paint with water until you have a thin creamy mixture. Using this mixture with a lining brush, paint a thin line about 2.5cm/1in to the right of each vertical green line. Leave to dry.

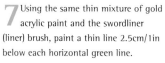

7 Using the same thin mixture of gold acrylic paint and the swordliner (liner) brush, paint a thin line 2.5cm/1in below each horizontal green line.

8 Paint the whole desk in a dark oak effect and leave to dry. Draw a large rectangle on the top and mask off. Apply a base coat of pale pink satinwood paint and leave to dry. Mix pale pink satinwood paint with powdered interior filler (casting plaster) until you have a paste-like mixture. Dab this mixture over the whole surface until it is about 1cm/½in thick.

9 Stipple over the whole surface with the tips of the bristles of the same household brush used in step 8, texturing the surface. Leave this to dry thoroughly.

10 Brush undiluted crimson artists' oil colour paint over the surface in a fairly thick coat. Stipple to even out, using the same brush as in step 9.

11 Using the flat side of a clean dry sponge, skim over the surface very gently. Apply no pressure but just let the sponge sit on the surface, removing some of the oil from the top layer and highlighting the whole texture. Varnish when dry.

RIGHT: The deep colours chosen for the tartan (plaid) border complement and provide a contrast for the walls of the study, creating a co-ordinated scheme. Borders and bands of checks can define the shape of a room. Placing a horizontal border immediately under the window helps to emphasize the width of the room.

SANTA FE LIVING ROOM

A ztec motifs, like this bird, are bold, stylized and one-dimensional, and translate perfectly into stamps. Strong colour contrasts suit this style, but here the pattern is confined to widely spaced stripes over a cool white wall, and further restrained with white paint dry brushed over the stamped motifs.

You will need

- matt emulsion (latex) paint in off-white, antique white, deep red and navy blue
- paint-mixing container
- natural sponge
- broad and medium paintbrushes
- plumb line
- ruler
- pencil
- masking tape
- marker pen
- medium-density sponge
- craft knife and cutting mat
- small paint roller
- old plate
- high-density foam rubber

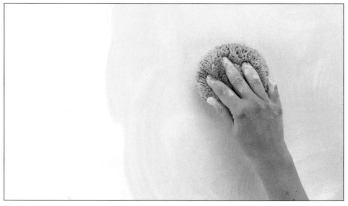

1 Dilute the off-white emulsion (latex) with 50 per cent water and, using a sponge, apply a wash over the wall in an overlapping circular motion. Allow to dry.

2 Using a broad, dry brush, apply warm white emulsion in some areas of the wall to achieve a rough-looking surface. Allow to dry.

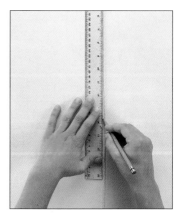

3 Starting 10cm/4in from one corner, and using a plumb line as a guide, draw a straight line from the top to the bottom of the wall.

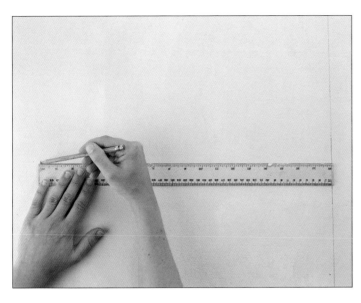

4 Measure 45cm/18in along the wall, hang the plumbline again and mark a second vertical line. Draw another line 10cm/4in away to create a band. Repeat all across the wall.

5 Apply masking tape to the wall on each outer edge of the marked bands.

6 Paint the bands in deep red emulsion (latex) paint. Leave to dry.

7 Draw a 10 x 20cm/4 x 8in diamond shape on a medium-density sponge and cut out the shape using a craft knife and cutting mat.

8 Use a small roller to load the stamp with navy blue emulsion (latex) paint and stamp the diamonds down the red bands, starting from the top. Re-coat for each stamp.

9 Copy the bird template at the back of the book on to a piece of high-density foam rubber. Cut away the excess sponge using a craft knife.

10 Use the roller to load the bird stamp with off-white emulsion (latex) and print the birds upright, roughly in the centre of the diamonds.

11 When the motifs are dry, use minimal pressure and a dry brush to brush gently over each band with warm white emulsion (latex) paint.

RIGHT: The paint effects are combined with wooden furniture to complete this look.

JAPANESE LIVING ROOM

Roller fidgeting is used to create the warm-looking walls of this traditional Japanese-style living room. Two paint colours mix and merge on the wall as they are applied, providing an ideal ground for a simple freehand leaf design. Painted bamboo panels worked in richer artists' oil colours add an air of authenticity and are fun to paint. Finally the furniture is given a smooth lacquered finish to complement the setting.

You will need

- emulsion (latex) paint in off-white, sand yellow, pale cream and plum
- wide household paintbrush
- masonry paint roller
- roller tray
- pencil
- fine artist's brush
- satin or gloss finish paint in pale yellow
- artists' oil colour paint in yellow ochre and burnt umber
- white spirit (turpentine)
- small paint kettle (pot)
- tape measure
- fine lining brush
- coffee table
- fine-grade sandpaper
- gloss finish paint in plum
- spray gloss enamel in plum
- spray gloss varnish

1 Apply a coat of off-white emulsion (latex) paint to the wall and leave to dry thoroughly.

2 Pour sand yellow and pale cream emulsion (latex) paint into each side of a roller tray. Coat a masonry roller with the paint and apply it to the wall at random angles, making sure that you do not totally cover the base coat.

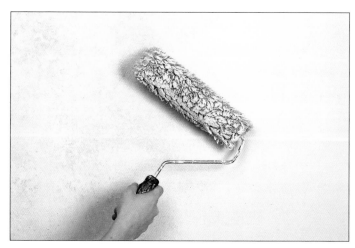

3 When the wall is dry mark with a pencil the height and position of the leaf spray border design. Take into account the width of the bamboo panels which will alternate between the leaves. Draw these in at the same time. Draw the centre lines, making sure they are equally spaced around the room, then draw in the leaves freehand.

4 Use an artist's brush to paint in the main stalk in plum emulsion (latex).

5 Paint in the leaves in plum emulsion (latex) paint. Some parts of the leaf spray design may need a second coat.

6 Mask off each of the panels. Apply two coats of pale yellow satin or gloss finish paint and leave to dry thoroughly. Mix yellow ochre artists' oil colour paint with white spirit (turpentine) into a creamy consistency in a small paint kettle (pot). Drag the mixture over the surface. Leave this to dry thoroughly.

7 Measure and draw pencil lines about 1.25cm/½in apart in the direction of the dragging. Once the pencil lines are complete, draw in the slightly rounded ends of the bamboo. Make sure there are not too many of these or it will look far too complicated when finished.

8 Mix burnt umber artists' oil colour paint with white spirit (turpentine) in a paint kettle (pot) to make a thick cream. Using a fine lining brush, draw over the pencil lines adding elongated lines from the middle of the bamboo ends about 12.5cm/5in long. Flick tiny dots of the paint over the surface, and soften with the edge of a brush, moving downwards.

9 To prepare the surface of the table, first sand it thoroughly until totally smooth. Clean the surface, making sure that it is completely free of dust. Apply a base coat of high gloss paint and leave to dry thoroughly. Sand the surface again to ensure total smoothness.

10 Apply a second base coat. Leave to dry thoroughly.

11 Spray on a gloss enamel in the same colour as the base coat. Again, leave to dry thoroughly. Spray a gloss varnish over the surface to protect it and provide a final finish.

RIGHT: The table is lacquered in plum-coloured paint to match the leaf design on the walls. This colour provides a sophisticated contrast to the warm creamy yellow of the walls and darker ochre tones of the bamboo panel without looking too overpowering.

COLONIAL LIVING ROOM

One of the easiest methods for creating a wood panel effect is to use the technique of dragging. Simply pull the wet paint with the tips of the bristles of a dry brush in the direction of the wood grain. The technique creates maximum impact in rooms where large areas of panelling are required, such as this Colonial-style living room. It is important to keep the lines in each vertical or horizontal section clean and unbroken, so make sure you plan panels that can be covered with a comfortable stroke of the brush.

You will need

◆ emulsion (latex) paint in off-white and
  mid (medium) brown
◆ household paintbrush
◆ long ruler
◆ pencil
◆ masking tape
◆ wallpaper paste
◆ paint kettle (pot)
◆ soft artist's brush
◆ cloth

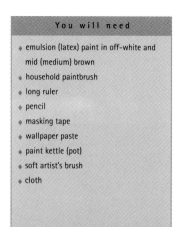

1 Apply two coats of off-white emulsion (latex) paint over the whole wall. Leave to dry. Measure and mark the height and size of the panelling you require with the ruler and pencil. Make sure the proportions balance well across the length of the wall.

2 Mask off the dado (chair) rail. Mix mid brown emulsion (latex) paint with 50 per cent wallpaper paste in a paint kettle (pot). Brush the paint mixture over the dado (chair) rail area. Using a dry brush, drag along the middle of the rail in a horizontal direction to remove some of the paint and create a highlight effect. Apply masking tape to the borders of the main panels, mitring the corners, then paint and drag the centre panel in a vertical direction.

3 Mask off the top and bottom sections, and paint and then drag them in a horizontal direction.

4 Remove the tape except from the centre panel border. Brush the brown paint mixture on to the side panels and drag down in a vertical direction. Leave the paint to dry.

LEFT: *Masking with mitred edges enables you to drag right up to the corners with precision. The highlights and shadows give the illusion of depth. You can achieve the effect easily by mitring the masking tape before applying it, then removing it length by length as you paint each edge.*

5 Remove the tape from the bottom of the centre panels and paint in a second coat of the brown mixture to give a darker shadow effect, using a soft artist's brush. Repeat the process for the right-hand side (assuming the light source is from the left).

6 Remove the tape from the left of the centre panels and paint in a coat of the brown mixture, dragging the brush along the inner edge. To create a highlight, take a cloth, while the paint is still damp, wrap it over your index finger and run this along the band removing most of the paint. Repeat the process for the top side (assuming the light source is coming in from the left).

RIGHT: Leather furniture and dark wooden accessories perfectly complement the effect of the wood panels, further enhancing the authenticity of the colonial setting.

SEASIDE KITCHEN

Bring the look of happy seaside vacations into your kitchen throughout the year. The wall is colourwashed using two layers of the same colour to produce an effective backdrop of movement and depth. Simple beach flag motifs are stamped on the wall in a casual manner to reflect the coastal theme, and details painted in with a small brush. The flaking paint on the cupboard is the result of applying a crackle-glaze medium between the two layers of colour on the panels and dry brushing.

1 Apply a base coat of white emulsion (latex) paint to the wall. Leave to dry. Mix mid (medium) blue emulsion (latex) paint with 50 per cent wallpaper paste in a paint kettle (pot). Apply the mixture to the wall at random angles using a broad decorator's brush and allowing the base coat to show through.

2 When the first layer of blue colourwash is dry, apply a second coat, again in random directions.

3 Using a mini roller, apply a good coat of white emulsion (latex) paint to the raised surface of the stamp.

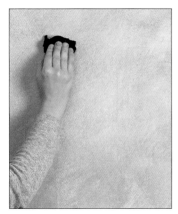

4 Decide where you are going to place the stamp, position it and then press firmly on the wall.

5 Continue to apply stamps to the wall, placing them randomly and making sure that one motif is not directly positioned directly in line with another.

6 When you have completed the stamping use an artist's brush to paint the flagpoles in yellow emulsion (latex) paint to complete the motifs.

7 To decorate the cupboard, apply two base coats of mid (medium) blue emulsion (latex) paint to the outside. Leave to dry.

RIGHT: Cupboards and other small items of furniture are easy to treat with a crackle-glaze effect. Use it to reproduce surfaces that are reminiscent of beach huts exposed to salt and the extremes of the elements through rain and shine.

8 When the blue paint is dry, apply a good coat of crackle-glaze medium to the centre panel, following the manufacturer's instructions.

9 Paint a good coat of white emulsion (latex) over the area where you applied the crackle-glaze medium. Do not overbrush, since the medium will react with the paint fairly quickly to produce the crackle effect. Leave to dry upright to achieve a dramatic cracking effect.

10 Complete the surround to the cupboard panel by scraping the excess white paint from the brush and dry brushing along the edging in the direction of the grain of the wood.

RIGHT: *The seaside theme is continued in the accessories in the kitchen, with bright striped china and wooden boats. Plain white shelving can be given an antiqued effect or made from leftover pieces of wood that have been washed up on the shore.*

MANHATTAN DINING ROOM

This minimalist, yet striking, striped wall provides an interesting backdrop to a room that is a haven away from the hubbub of city life. The impact of these wide stripes is maximized by taking them right over the skirting (base) board to floor level. A plain beech effect is used to paint the table top, and the surface pattern and texture is achieved by using a heart grainer (graining roller) and comb. The techniques are easy to master. Finally, remember to varnish the table to protect your handiwork.

1 Apply two coats of off-white emulsion (latex) paint to the wall. Leave the paint to dry completely.

2 Using a long ruler and spirit level (level), measure 30cm/12in wide stripes, marking them out with a pencil.

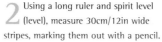

3 Paint in alternate bands using a wide paint pad and taupe emulsion (latex) paint. Concentrate on the edges before filling the inside of the bands. The paint pad should be well coated, but not over loaded. Press firmly whle pulling down the pencil line to achieve an accurate line.

4 To paint the beech-effect table, apply two coats of white satinwood paint as a base coat. Leave each to dry before applying the next. Mix Naples yellow artists' oil colour paint with white spirit (turpentine) until you have a mixture the consistency of thick cream, then brush it evenly over the surface.

5 Drag the surface in a single, lengthways direction.

6 Use a heart grainer (graining roller) to start making the graining. Do this by pulling the tool down gently, slightly rocking it and working in several spaced lines. Do not butt the lines up together.

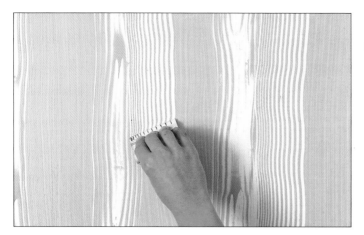

7 With a graduated comb, work in the same direction and fill in the lines between the heart graining.

8 Again, working in the same direction, soften the effect with a large dry brush.

9 Now take a narrow comb and go over the entire surface in the same direction to add detail to the effect. Repeat this until fine lines are achieved. Varnish when dry.

RIGHT: *Beech is a light-coloured wood much used for modern furniture and this effect tones well with the stripes on the wall. Although all the colours are neutral in this room, they are varied and warm looking. Choose simple shapes for accessories to enhance the overall contemporary look.*

PROVENÇAL KITCHEN

This kitchen is a dazzling example of contrasting colours – the effect is almost electric. Colours opposite each other in the colour wheel give the most vibrant contrast and you could equally well experiment with a combination of blue and orange or red and green. If, however, these colours are just too vivid for you, then choose a gentler colour scheme with the same stamped pattern. The kitchen walls are colourwashed to give a mottled, patchy background. Put some wallpaper paste in the colourwash to make the job a lot easier – it also prevents too many streaks from running down the walls.

You will need

♦ emulsion (latex) paint in deep purple and
  pale yellow
♦ wallpaper paste (made up according to
  the manufacturer's instructions)
♦ paintbrush
♦ plumb line
♦ cardboard measuring approximately
  30cm x 30cm/12in x 12in
♦ pencil
♦ plates for palettes
♦ foam rollers
♦ rosebud and small rose stamps
♦ acrylic paint in red and green
♦ clear matt varnish and brush

1 To make the colourwash, mix one part deep purple emulsion (latex) with one part wallpaper paste and four parts water. Make it up in multiples of six. It is best to make more than you need. Then colourwash the walls. If runs occur, just pick them up with the brush and work them into the surrounding wall, aiming for a patchy, mottled effect.

2 Attach the plumb line at ceiling height, just in from the corner. Hold the cardboard square against the wall so that the string cuts through the top and bottom corners. Mark all four points with a pencil. Continue moving the square and marking points to make a grid pattern.

3 Spread some deep purple paint on to the plate and run the roller through it until it is evenly coated. Ink the rosebud stamp and print a rosebud on each pencil mark until you have covered the wall.

4 If you wish to create a dropped-shadow effect, clean the stamp and spread some pale yellow paint on to the plate. Ink the stamp and over-print each rosebud, moving the stamp so that it is slightly off register.

5 Continue over-printing the rosebuds, judging by eye the position of the yellow prints.

BELOW: Attach a wooden peg rail to the patterned walls to match the Provençal theme.

6 For the cupboard doors apply a base coat in pale yellow. Spread some green and burnt orange paint on to the plates and run the rollers through them until they are evenly coated. Coat the rose with burnt orange and the leaves with green. (If one colour mixes with the other, just wipe it off and re-coat.) Print a rose in the top left-hand corner. Re-coat the stamp for each print.

7 Print the stamp horizontally and vertically to make a border along the edges of the door panel.

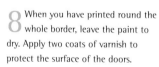

8 When you have printed round the whole border, leave the paint to dry. Apply two coats of varnish to protect the surface of the doors.

RIGHT: The stamping on the walls and the cupboards instantly transforms a plain kitchen into a busy working one, conjuring up images of delicious French dishes.

RENAISSANCE HALLWAY

Turn your hallway into a dramatic entrance with ornate stencils and rich colours inspired by Renaissance designs. The sponged background is a useful device for creating an illusion of texture to the walls and is in keeping with the ornate look of this scheme. Combine the paint effects on the walls with gold accessories, velvets and braids to complete the theatrical setting. This design would also be ideal for creating an intimate dining room for candlelit dinners, with its warm, romantic colours punctuated by luxurious finishing touches seen in the gilded furniture and refined fabric.

You will need

- ruler
- spirit level (level)
- pencil
- masking tape
- emulsion (latex) paints in pale slate-blue, terracotta and pale peach
- sponges
- stencil brushes
- stencil card (card stock)
- craft knife and cutting mat
- stencil paints in dark grey-blue, terracotta, emerald and turquoise

1 Using a ruler and spirit level (level), divide the wall in half horizontally with a pencil line, then draw a second line 15cm/6in above the first. Stick a line of masking tape just below this top line. Dilute one part slate-blue emulsion (latex) with one part water and colour the top half of the wall using a sponge.

2 Stick masking tape just above the bottom pencil line. Dilute terracotta emulsion (latex) paint with water and sponge over the lower half of the wall.

3 Sponge lightly over the terracotta with slate-blue to add a textural effect. Remove the strips of masking tape once you have covered the whole of the wall.

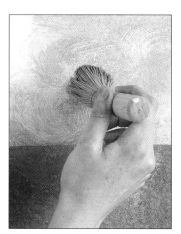

ABOVE: If you are feeling very ambitious, make a matching patchwork cushion cover using pieces of fabric stencilled with gold fabric paint.

4 Colour the centre band with diluted peach emulsion using a stencil brush. Trace the templates at the back of the book and cut out the stencils from stencil card.

5 Stencil the wall motifs at roughly regular intervals over the upper part of the
wall, using dark grey-blue. Rotate the stencil with every alternate motif to give
movement to the design.

6 Starting at the right-hand side of the peach band, stencil the border motif
with terracotta stencil paint. Add details in emerald and turquoise. Continue
along the wall, positioning the stencil beside the previous motif so that the spaces
are equal, creating a balanced effect.

*RIGHT: Complete the look with an ornate brass candle holder, fixed to a plain section
of wall, between the stencils.*

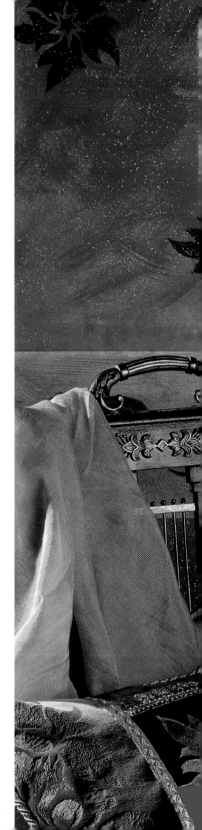

SCANDINAVIAN DOOR PANELS

Painted furniture and fittings are very popular in Scandinavia, especially designs that celebrate nature. These beautiful panels are painted freehand, with flowing brushstrokes. Do not worry too much about making the doors symmetrical – it is more important that the painting should look natural. Practise the strokes with art brushes first on a piece of paper until you feel confident. Any cupboard or dresser doors would be suitable for this design. You could even decorate modern kitchen units.

You will need

- pale yellow emulsion (latex) paint – ochre rather than lemon
- medium decorator's paintbrush
- plant and flowerpot design
- pencil
- artist's acrylic paint in yellow ochre, ultramarine and antique white
- old white plates
- lining brush
- rounded artist's brush
- clear matt varnish and brush

1 Paint the door panels with pale yellow emulsion (latex). Leave to dry. Draw the design on each panel in pencil, using the template at the back of the book.

2 Put some yellow ochre artist's acrylic paint on to a plate. Mix in ultramarine to make grey-green. Using a lining brush, begin painting the design at the top of the first panel.

3 Work your way down the panel, resting your painting hand on your other hand to keep it steady.

4 Put some antique white artist's
acrylic paint on to a plate. Using an
artist's brush, paint the flowerpot and
swirls below. Add the flowers, applying
pressure to the brush. Darken the paint
with more yellow ochre, then add the soil
colouring in the pot.

5 Paint the other panel and leave to
dry. Apply a protective coat of clear
matt varnish.

*RIGHT: Use this design on a cupboard to
create a country theme in a kitchen.*

MEDIEVAL HALLWAY

A welcoming hallway decorated with medieval patterns and colours will make a stunning entrance to your home. If your hallway seems dark and narrow, using two colours will help make it appear more spacious. A dark colour above dado (chair) rail height creates the illusion of a lower ceiling, while a light colour below, combined with a light floor covering, seems to push the walls outwards to give the impression of width. The crown pattern on the lower half of the wall is stamped in a diagonal grid, which is easy to draw using a plumb line and a square of card (card stock).

1 Draw a horizontal pencil line on the wall, at dado (chair) rail height. Paint the top half in blue-green and the bottom in buttermilk yellow emulsion (latex) paint. When dry, lightly sand the blue-green paint. Stick a strip of masking tape along the lower edge of the blue-green, and another 10cm/4in below. Apply light cream paint with a dry roller over the buttermilk yellow.

2 Stick another length of masking tape 2cm/5in below the one marking the edge of the blue-green section. Using a paintbrush and blue-green paint, fill in the stripe between the two lower strips of tape. Leave to dry and peel off the tape. Lightly sand the blue-green stripe to give it the appearance of the upper section of wall.

3 On a plate, mix one part blue-green emulsion (latex) paint with two parts pre-mixed wallpaper paste and stir well. Ink the diamond stamp with the foam roller and stamp a row of diamonds on the narrow cream stripe.

BELOW: *Basic geometric patterns used at dado (chair) rail height are a useful decorative device to separate the different background colours, above and below.*

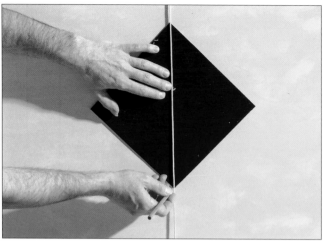

4 Use a plumb line and a card (card stock) square to mark an all-over grid on the cream half of the wall. This will be used as a guide for the crown stamps.

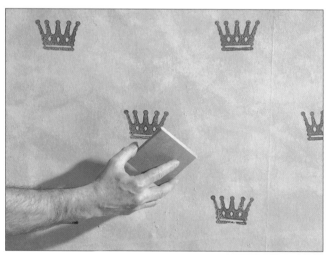

5 Ink the crown stamp with the blue-green emulsion (latex) paint and wallpaper paste mixture and stamp a motif on each pencil mark. Make several prints before re-inking to create variation in the density of the prints.

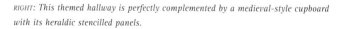

RIGHT: This themed hallway is perfectly complemented by a medieval-style cupboard with its heraldic stencilled panels.

MEXICAN HALLWAY

Banish gloomy weather with vibrant sunshine yellow and intense sky blue in your hallway. With the heat turned up, add an ethnic touch by stamping an Aztec border along the walls. Use the patterns from the template section to cut basic geometric shapes from a foam rubber sponge, such as the ones used for washing dishes. Mix shades of green with purples, add an earthy red and then stamp on diamonds of fuchsia pink for its sheer brilliance. This makes a bold decorative statement.

Emulsion (latex) paint is available in a wide range of exciting colours. Try not to be tempted by muted colours for this border – it will lose much of its impact. Bright colours go well with natural materials, like straw hats, sisal matting, wicker baskets and clay pots.

You will need

- tape measure
- spirit level (level)
- pencil
- emulsion (latex) paint in sunshine yellow and deep sky blue
- paint roller and tray
- small amounts of emulsion (latex) paint in light blue-grey, purple, brick-red, fuchsia pink and dark green
- 5 plates
- foam rubber sponge

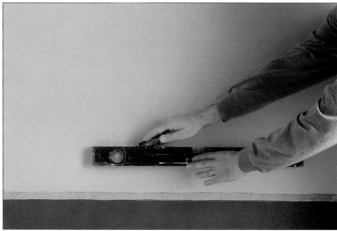

1 Divide the wall at dado (chair) rail height using a tape measure, spirit level (level) and pencil. Paint the upper part in sunshine yellow and the lower part in deep sky blue, using a paint roller. Then use the spirit level (level) and pencil to draw a parallel line about 15cm/6in above the blue section.

2 Use the templates from the back of the book to make the foam rubber stamps for this project. Then stamp a light blue-grey line directly above the blue section. Use this strip again to stamp the top line of the border along the pencil line.

3 Spread an even coating of each of the frieze colours on to separate plates. Use the rectangular and triangular shapes alternately to print a purple row above the bottom line and below the top line. Stamp on to a piece of scrap paper first to make sure that the stamp is not overloaded.

4 Stamp the largest shape in brick red, lining it up to fit between the points of the top and bottom triangles. There should be approximately 1.25cm/½in of background colour showing between this brick-red shape and the triangles.

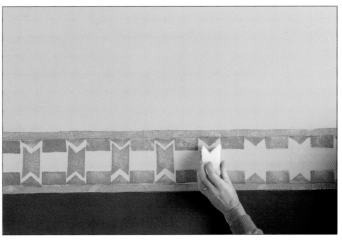

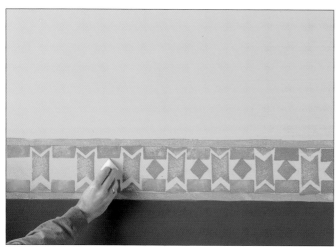

5 Stamp the diamond shapes in fuchsia pink, placing the stamps centrally between the brick-red motifs already stamped.

6 Finally, add a zigzagged edge along the top and bottom by overprinting dark green triangles along the light blue-grey lines.

RIGHT: The rustic wooden furniture adds an authentic touch to this Mexican setting.

POTTING SHED

reate the relaxing atmosphere of a rural potting shed in a hallway where you keep all the clutter needed for use in the garden. Here, broken-colour techniques are used, adding layers of paint to produce a gentle, muted look to the surroundings. The wall is dry brushed in a downward dragging motion to give a softly textured effect. Four layers of colours are used to give depth to the effect as each coat is allowed to show through. The window box and the individual plant pots are given a verdigris finish to make them stylish for decorative use.

You will need

- emulsion (latex) paint in white, cream, moss green and sage green
- large household paintbrush
- paint kettle (pot)
- window box
- sandpaper
- satin or gloss finish paint in jade green
- enamel paint in bronze and gold
- gilt cream in copper
- polishing cloth

1 Apply a base coat of white emulsion (latex) paint to the wall and leave to dry. Dip the tip of a large household paintbrush into cream emulsion (latex) paint, scrape off the excess and apply to the wall in long vertical strokes. Vary the starting point with each stroke and allow the base coat to show through. Leave to dry thoroughly.

2 Then, dip the tip of the paintbrush into moss green emulsion (latex) paint and scrape off the excess. Dry brush the paint on to the wall using long vertical strokes. Make sure that the layer of colour underneath shows through. Leave to dry.

3 Similarly, dry brush a layer of sage green emulsion (latex) paint using vertical strokes and allowing the underlayers to show through. Leave to dry thoroughly.

4 Finally, when dry, dry brush a layer of cream emulsion (latex) paint in a similar manner to steps 2 and 3.

RIGHT: Dry-brushed layers of soft greens and cream produce a gentle background that exudes calmness and tranquillity. Use this effect to turn an area of your home into a retreat away from the stresses of everyday life and a place to get in touch with nature by caring for plants.

5 To prepare the window box for decorating, rub down the surface with sandpaper to provide a key so that the paint will adhere. Apply a base coat of jade green satin or gloss finish paint and leave to dry thoroughly.

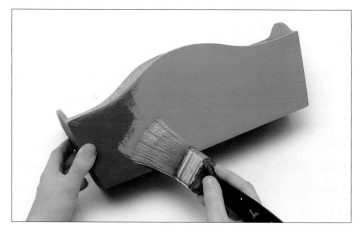

6 Lightly stipple bronze enamel paint over the surface using the tips of the bristles of the brush, making sure that you keep the base coat exposed.

7 Stipple gold enamel paint over the whole surface even more lightly than the bronze layer and in random patches.

8 With a dry brush, dab over the surface of the jade green base coat, blending slightly. Leave to dry. Rub a little copper gilt cream over the whole surface with the tips of the brush. Then, buff to a strong shine with a dry cloth.

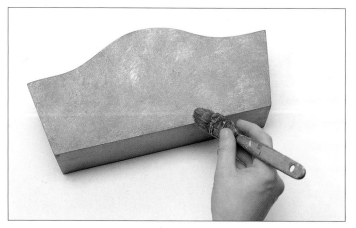

RIGHT: The colours used in this arrangement are kept light and are enhanced by the harmoniously painted furniture and accessories.

CHURCH HALLWAY

Turn your hallway into a welcoming area of serenity by decorating the walls with a dressed-stone effect reminiscent of an old country church. This easy technique relies on precision in drawing a grid to mark out the individual blocks before painting them in. Consistent edges of highlight and shadow define the blocks. To emphasize the church-like look, the cupboard is painted with a dark oak effect. The rich depth of colour of solid oak is achieved by using burnt umber artists' oil colour paint.

You will need

- sponge
- emulsion (latex) paint in stone yellow, off-white and beige
- spirit level (level)
- pencil
- paint kettle (pot)
- wallpaper paste
- 1.25cm/½in flat end paintbrush
- wooden cupboard
- gloss or satin finish paint in beige
- artists' oil colour paint in burnt umber
- white spirit (turpentine)
- fine graduated comb
- heart grainer (graining roller)
- cloth
- large paintbrush
- varnish

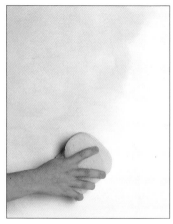

1 Dip a sponge into stone yellow emulsion (latex) and apply to the wall in a circular motion, creating an overall mottled effect.

2 Add a second coat of the stone yellow emulsion (latex) in patches and leave to dry. This will create a slight movement in the overall effect but will look almost solid.

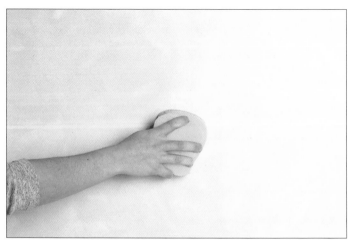

3 Using a spirit level (level), draw a grid simulating the blocks to achieve a straight and accurate grid for the stone blocking effect.

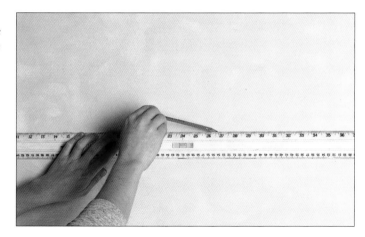

4 Mix off-white emulsion (latex) paint with 50 per cent wallpaper paste in a small paint kettle (pot). Using a 1.25cm/½in flat end paintbrush, paint a stroke across the top and right side of each block. Leave to dry.

5 Make sure the mitred corners are painted crisply.

6 Mix beige emulsion paint with 50 per cent wallpaper paste in a small paint kettle (pot). Use the same flat end paintbrush to paint along the bottom and left of each block. Mitre each corner which joins the highlight.

7 To paint the cupboard, apply two coats of beige for the base coat in either gloss or satin finish and leave to dry thoroughly. Mix burnt umber artists' oil colour paint with white spirit (turpentine) in a paint kettle (pot) until it is the consistency of thick cream. Brush on and drag in a lengthways direction.

8 Using a graduated comb, pull down on the surface, not in totally straight lines, butting one up against the other.

9 Use a heart grainer (graining roller) to start making the details of the graining. Do this by pulling the tool down gently with a slight rocking motion, to create the hearts with random spacings. Butt one line straight over the other. Using a fine graduated comb, comb over all the previous combing.

10 Wrap a cloth around the comb and dab on to the surface to create the angled grain, pressing into the wet paint. Then, soften the overall effect using a large dry brush. Varnish when dry.

RIGHT: *Enhance the church-like effect of the dressed-stone blocking by adding a formal flower arrangement and accessories such as old leather-bound books. Plain church candles are readily available and give a gentle glow at night when lit.*

EGYPTIAN BATHROOM

Here, a roller fidgeting technique is ideal for establishing the impression of a slightly textured surface and disguising any small imperfections in the plaster. This bathroom is decorated with Egyptian fan motifs that are carefully measured and drawn before being painted in. The shapes are masked to make painting them in easier and then outlined with paint to make them stand out clearly. Decoration within the motifs is made with a comb while the paint is still wet.

You will need

♦ emulsion (latex) paint in pale yellow,
  off-white, orange and turquoise
♦ wallpaper paste
♦ paint kettle (pot)
♦ large paintbrush
♦ pencil
♦ long ruler
♦ drawing pin
♦ string
♦ masking tape
♦ rubber or plastic comb
♦ lining brush

1 Roller fidget the background using pale yellow and off-white in the same way. When dry, mark out the fan shapes in pencil. Do this with the aid of a long ruler, measuring and marking either side of a centre vertical line. Secure a piece of string to the centre line with a drawing pin and attach the pencil to the other end to draw an arc for the top of the fan. Similarly measure and mark the smaller half fans.

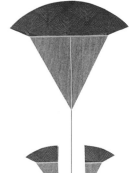

2 Carefully mask off the lower part of each fan (the triangular shape) with masking tape and brush over the enclosed area with a layer of orange emulsion (latex) paint.

3 Immediately, and before the paint has dried, comb over the orange colour in a downwards vertical direction, keeping your hand steady so that the lines are straight. Leave to dry.

4 Mask off the top part of each fan and brush over with turquoise emulsion (latex) paint, until the enclosed area is completely covered.

5 Again, comb immediately. To achieve the semi-circle patterns, start by angling the comb and your wrist on the left and arc with the top, without moving the bottom of the comb. Leave to dry.

6 Mix some off-white emulsion (latex) paint with a little water until you have a thin creamy mixture. Use this mixture with a lining brush to paint a thin line around all the coloured shapes to clean up any untidy edges. Finally, paint in the centre line of the large fans and the supporting lines of the half fans.

RIGHT: These Egyptian fan motifs are painted in the typical colours of orange and turquoise used by the ancient Pharaohs. These colours were originally made from natural clays and minerals, and their earthy tones are complemented by the pale yellow colourwashed wall. The vibrant look is completed with the addition of colourful shutters and bright accessories.

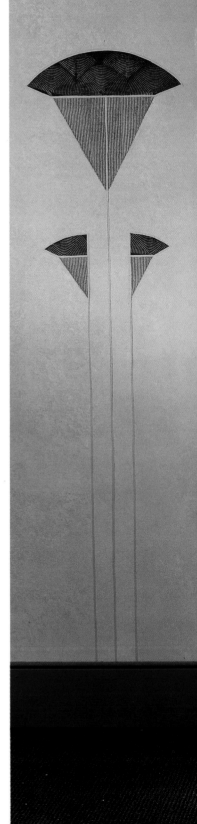

STAR BATHROOM

This misty blue colour scheme is ideal for a bathroom or staircase because the lower part of the wall is varnished to provide a practical wipe-clean surface. The tinted varnish deepens the colour and gives it a sheen that contrasts well with the chalky distemper (tempera) above. The stencil is a traditional quilting motif.

You will need

- tracing paper and pencil
- scissors
- spray adhesive
- stencil card (card stock)
- sharp craft knife and cutting mat
- soft blue distemper (tempera) or chalk-based paint
- large decorator's paintbrushes
- straightedge
- spirit level (level)
- clear satin water-based varnish
- Prussian blue artist's acrylic paint

1 Trace the star from the back of the book and cut out. Spray the back with adhesive and stick to the card.

2 Using a craft knife, cut out the star. Cut inwards from the points towards the centre so that the points stay crisp.

3 Taking a corner first, carefully peel away the paper template on the top to reveal the stencil underneath.

4 Dilute the paint, if necessary, according to the manufacturer's instructions. Brush it on to the wall with sweeping, random strokes to give a colourwashed effect.

5 Using a straightedge and spirit level (level), draw a pencil line across the wall at the height you want to end the darker varnished surface.

6 Tint the varnish with a squeeze of Prussian blue acrylic paint. Using a separate brush, apply this on the lower part of the wall up to the marked line.

7 Spray the back of the stencil with adhesive and position at one end of the wall, 5cm/2in above the marked line. Stencil with the tinted varnish, using a broad sweep of the brush. Repeat along the wall, spacing the stars evenly.

RIGHT: A classic geometric eight-pointed star is a beautifully simple decoration.

NEO-CLASSICAL BATHROOM

After a hard day's work, transport yourself to the relaxing atmosphere of the ancient Roman baths but with all the conveniences of modern living. This old cast-iron bath (bath tub) is painted with a marble effect on the outside that is easy to achieve, with enamel paint used as a base coat. Use a swordliner (liner) or feather to paint in veins, then soften them off for a realistic subtle look. The wall panels are given a light trompe l'oeil sky effect, so that you have the impression of looking through columns or open window spaces to the exhilarating fresh air outside.

You will need

- cast-iron bath (bath tub)
- suitable enamel paint in white
- household paintbrush
- artists' oil colour paint in Davy's grey (medium gray)
- white spirit (turpentine)
- paint kettle (pot)
- swordliner (liner) or feather
- large softener (blending) brush
- varnish in gloss finish
- emulsion (latex) paint in white and sky blue
- silk finish emulsion (latex) paint in white
- sponge and pencil
- wallpaper paste

1 To decorate the bath tub, apply two coats of white enamel paint to the outer surface of it.

2 Mix a little Davy's grey (medium gray) artists' oil colour paint with white spirit (turpentine) in a small paint kettle (pot) until it has a thin creamy consistency. Use this mixture to paint in the fine veins of the marble with a swordliner (liner) or a feather.

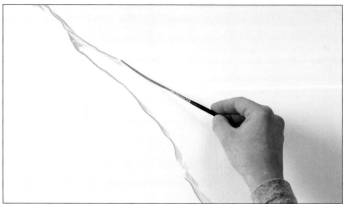

3 Soften the veins using a large soft brush to sweep over the lines.

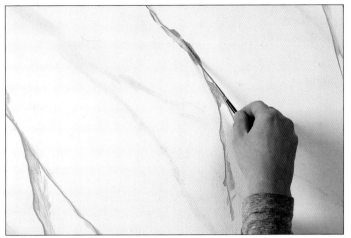

4 Add more veins, disregarding the positions of the first ones but working in the same general direction.

5 Soften these new veins with the large soft brush using only a little pressure this time, to give these ones a slightly stronger edge.

6 Using the swordliner (liner), add a defining line along the side of the second set of veins. Pull the softening brush along these once if slightly heavy. Leave to dry. Varnish in a gloss finish.

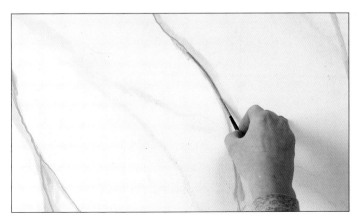

7 To paint the walls, apply two coats of white emulsion (latex) as a base coat, allowing to dry between coats. Measure, draw and mask off the panels. Dip a sponge into sky blue emulsion (latex) paint and rub over the panel in a circular motion, leaving a mottled effect. Once dry, apply a second coat of sky blue with a sponge in the same way. The second coat will leave the whole effect almost solid but slightly mottled in appearance.

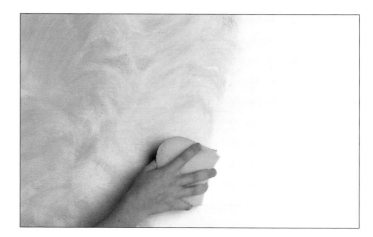

8 Using a light pencil, carefully outline rough cloud shapes to give a guide for painting.

9 Dilute white silk emulsion (latex) paint with 50 per cent wallpaper paste in a paint kettle (pot) and stipple this on to the surface, starting along the top edge of the pencil line. Continue to stipple downwards without applying any more paint to the brush and this will gradate the colour. Build up the depth of the clouds in layers when each has dried: go over the first layer along the top side and again stipple downwards. This will strengthen the effect.

10 Finally add a sharper edge to define the white.

RIGHT: This wonderful trompe l'oeil sky is glimpsed through window shapes and adds the illusion of space to the bathroom. Try it also on ceilings. The luminous quality is achieved by working down the surface several times, gradating the colour as you progress without adding more paint to the brush.

SCANDINAVIAN BEDROOM

This delicate stamped decoration on walls and woodwork has been applied with a very light touch and is designed to blend in with the pale coloured background and painted furniture so typical of period Scandinavian interiors.

1 Mix the grey-blue emulsion (latex) paint with 50 per cent wallpaper paste and apply to the walls with a broad paintbrush, working at random angles and blending the brushstrokes to avoid hard edges. Allow to dry, then repeat so as to soften the effect.

2 Mix 25 per cent off-white emulsion (latex) paint with 75 per cent wallpaper paste and brush on to the walls as before. Allow to dry.

3 Hang a plumb line 2.5cm/1in from one corner and use as a guide to draw a vertical line down the wall. Measure about 40cm/16in across and draw a second vertical line, again using the plumb line as a guide. Repeat all around the room.

4 Trace the template at the back of the book and transfer it to a rectangle of high-density foam rubber. Cut away the excess sponge around the design using a craft knife.

5 Use a small paint roller to load the stamp with off-white emulsion (latex) paint. Distribute the paint over the whole stamp.

6 Add details in red and grey-blue emulsion (latex) paint, using a paintbrush to add the colours over the off-white paint.

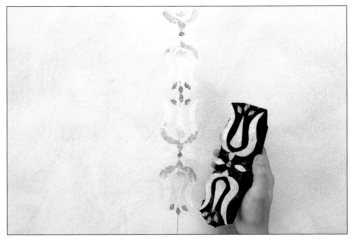

7 Apply the stamp to the wall, positioning it centrally over the marked line. Use the central red tip as a guide. Repeat, positioning the stamp so that each motif is just touching the preceding one. Work down from the top of the wall.

8 Use the grey-blue wash mixed for the wall base coat to drag the door. Do this by applying pressure to the bristles, then pulling down steadily in a straight line, following the direction of the wood grain as you go.

9 Apply the paint to the stamp as before, but this time loading only one flower motif. Stamp a single motif diagonally into the corners of each door panel.

10 Add more paint to the grey-blue wash to deepen the colour and use it to edge the door panels. Leave to dry, then apply two coats of matt varnish to the door to protect the design.

RIGHT: This charming scheme is perfect for the bedroom, creating a restful atmosphere.

COUNTRY QUILT FRIEZE

S tamp this friendly, folk-style frieze in a child's bedroom in soft pinks and a warm green.
The pattern is reminiscent of an old-fashioned appliqué quilt, and the overlapping edges
and jauntily angled birds accentuate its naïve charm. The colour scheme avoids the harshness
of primaries, which are so often chosen for children. Green is a calming colour, but it can be
cold. For this project use a sap green, which contains a lot of yellow, for warmth. The finished
effect is bright enough to be eye-catching without overpowering.

You will need

◆ emulsion (latex) or artist's acrylic paint in
  green, sap green, pink and crimson
◆ paintbrushes
◆ pencil
◆ ruler
◆ spirit level (level)
◆ tracing paper
◆ spray adhesive
◆ medium-density sponge, such as a
  kitchen sponge
◆ craft knife
◆ 4 plates for paint palettes

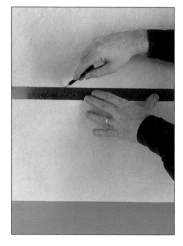

1 Divide the wall by painting the lower
section green, up to dado (chair) rail
height. Measure 24cm/9½in up from the
green section and draw a straight line
using a pencil, ruler and spirit level (level)
to act as a guide for the top border.

2 Trace the pattern shapes using the
templates from the back of the
book, then spray the backs with a light
coating of adhesive. Stick them on to the
foam and cut out with a craft knife.
Press the straight strip into green paint
and make a test print. Print a line along
the pencil guideline, and another just
above the green wall section.

3 Press the curved strip into the green paint, make a test print, then stamp curved lines to form a branch shape.

4 Press the leaf shape into the green paint, make a test print, then stamp the leaves in groups, as shown, two above and one below the branch.

BELOW: *This charming frieze would work equally well in a playroom. Since the design is not too babyish it will last throughout early childhood.*

5 Stamp pale pink birds along the branch – you need two prints, one facing each
direction. Do not make the prints too uniform; aim for a patchy effect.

6 Clean the sponges, then press them into the crimson paint. Stamp the rest of
the birds along the branch, alternating the direction of the motif as before.

7 Stamp a row of pink and crimson hearts above the top line to complete the
border pattern.

RIGHT: The colours used on the walls are echoed on the door panel, which is painted
freehand with a floral design, in keeping with the country theme.

INDIAN BEDHEAD

The inspiration for this arch-shaped bedhead (head board) comes from Indian temple wall paintings. The bedroom feels as if it has been magically transported thousands of miles, but the real magic here comes in a simple pot of paint. Before painting the bedhead (head board), set the mood with a deep rust-coloured wash on the walls. If you can, use a water-based distemper (tempera) for an authentic powdery bloom. If you are using emulsion (latex) paint, thin it with water and use random brushstrokes for a patchy, mottled look. The arch is simply chalked on to the wall using a paper template.

You will need

- large roll of brown parcel wrap (packing paper)
- felt-tipped pen
- masking tape (optional)
- scissors
- spray adhesive
- chalk
- water-based paint in dark blue, bright blue and red
- plate and kitchen sponge
- emulsion (latex) paint in sandy cream
- medium and fine paintbrushes
- fine-grade sandpaper

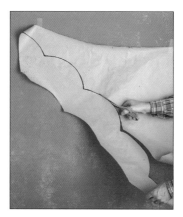

1 Tape a sheet of brown parcel wrap (packing paper) on the wall and draw the half-arch directly on to it, following the pattern shape. Cut out the half-arch shape using a pair of scissors.

2 Position the paper pattern on the wall with spray adhesive and draw around the edges with chalk.

3 Remove the pattern from the wall,
flip it over and position it on the
opposite side to produce the shape for
the second half of the arch. Draw around
the edges as before.

4 Spread some dark blue paint on to a
plate and use a damp sponge to dab
it on to the central panel. Do not cover
the background completely but leave
some of the wall colour showing
through. When the paint is dry, apply
the bright blue paint over the dark blue
in the same way.

5 When the paint is dry, paint the arch
in sandy cream emulsion, using a
medium-size paintbrush.

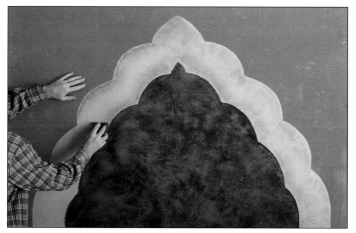

6 When the sandy cream paint is dry,
rub it back in places with fine-grade
sandpaper, to give a faded effect.

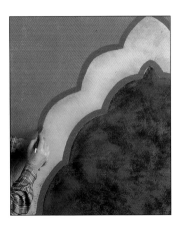

7 Outline the inside and outside of the arch with red paint, using a fine paintbrush. Support your painting hand with your other hand. Use the width of the brush to make a single line.

8 Outline the outer red stripe with a thinner dark blue line. Work as described in the previous step, keeping the line as clean as possible.

9 Leave to dry, then use fine-grade sandpaper to soften any hard edges so that the arch has the naturally faded appearance of an old temple wall.

RIGHT: A painted head board instantly tranforms the simplest of beds into an item of furniture with a definite style.

TEMPLATES

You can use these templates at this size or scale them up. Enlarge them on a photocopier, or trace the design and draw a grid of evenly spaced squares over your tracing. Draw a larger grid on another piece of paper and copy the outline square by square. Draw over the lines to make sure they are continuous.

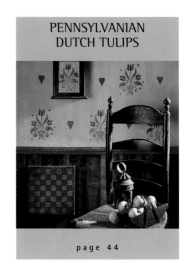

PENNSYLVANIAN DUTCH TULIPS

page 44

SANTA FE LIVING ROOM

page 52

SCANDINAVIAN LIVING ROOM

page 40

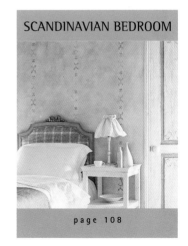

SCANDINAVIAN BEDROOM

page 108

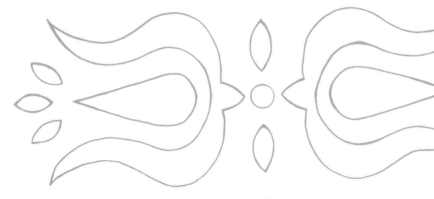

DOOR PANELS

page 80

COUNTRY QUILT FRIEZE

page 112

RENAISSANCE HALLWAY

page 76

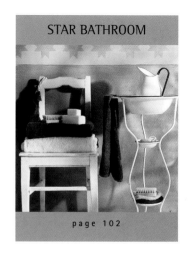

STAR BATHROOM

page 102

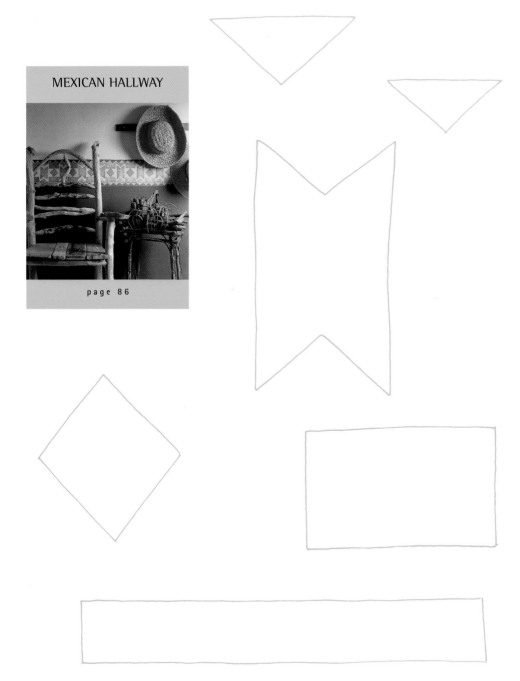

MEXICAN HALLWAY

page 86

SUPPLIERS

The speciality materials and equipment that you will require for the projects featured in this book are available at any good art-supply shop.

USA

Adventures in Crafts
Yorkwille Station
P.O. Box 6058
New York, NY 10128
(212) 410-9793

Art Essentials of New York Ltd
3 Cross Street
Suffern, NY 10901

Createx Colors
14 Ariport Park Road
East Granby, CT 06026
(860) 653-5505

Dick Blick
P.O. Box 1267
Galesburg, IL 61402
(309) 343-6181

Heartland Craft Discounters
Route 6 E., P.O. Box 65
Genesco, IL 61245
(309) 944-6411

Hofcraft
P.O. Box 72
Grand Haven, MI 49417
(800) 828-0359

Sandeen's
1315 White Bear Ave.
St. Paul, MN 55106
(612) 776-7012

Stencil House of New Hampshire
P.O. Box 16109
Hooksett, NH 03106
(603) 625-1716

UNITED KINGDOM

Blade Rubber Stamp Company
2 Neal's Yard
London
WC2H 9DP
(020) 7379 7391

Brodie and Middleton
68 Drury Lane
London
WC2B 5SP
(020) 7836 3289
Brushes, lacquer, metallic powders, oil and acrylic paints and powder pigments. Mail order.

Crown Paints
Crown Decorative Products Ltd
PO Box 37
Crown House
Hollins Road
Darwen
Lancashire

Do-it-all
(0800) 436 436 for stockists of paint and decorating materials.

Farrow and Ball
Uddens Estate
Wimbourne
Dorset BH21 7NL
Specialist paint suppliers.

Fired Earth
Twyford Mill
Oxford Road
Adderbury
Oxon OX17 3HP
Specialist paint suppliers.

Grand Illusions
2-4 Crown Road
St Margarets
Twickenham
Middlesex TW1 3EE
Specialist suppliers of materials used for paint effects.

Green and Stone
259 Kings Road
London
SW3 5EL
(020) 7352 0837
Brushes, crackle varnish, linseed oil, scumble glazes, shellac, and stencil card. Mail order.

Homebase
(0645) 801 800 for stockists of paint and decorating materials.

ICI Dulux
(01753) 550 555 for stockists of paint.

The Stamp Connection
14 Edith Road
Faversham
Kent ME13 8SD

Stuart Stevenson
68 Clerkenwell Road
London
EC1M 5QA
Gold and silver leaf and other gilding and art materials. Mail order.

Wickes
(0500) 300 328 for stockists of paint and decorating materials.

INDEX

ACKNOWLEDGEMENTS

The publishers would like to thank Foxell & James Ltd, of 57 Farringdon Road, London, for lending their equipment for photography, and the E.T archive for supplying the image on page 6.

NOTES

NOTES

NOTES

NOTES